To parents and teachers

We hope you and the children will enjoy reading this story in either English or Spanish. The story is simple, but not *simplified,* so that both versions are quite natural. However, there is plenty of repetition for practicing pronunciation, for helping develop memory skills, and for reinforcing comprehension.

At the back of the book is a small picture dictionary with the key words and how to pronounce them. There is also a simple pronunciation guide to the whole story on the last page.

Here are a few suggestions on using the book:

- Read the story aloud in English first, to get to know it. Treat it like any other picture book: look at the pictures, talk about the story and the characters, and so on.

- Then look at the picture dictionary and say the Spanish names for the key words. Ask the children to repeat them. Concentrate on speaking the words out loud, rather than reading them.

- Go back and read the story again, this time in English *and* Spanish. Don't worry if your pronunciation isn't quite correct. Just have fun trying it out. Check the guide at the back of the book, if necessary, but you'll soon pick up how to say the Spanish words.

- When you think you and the children are ready, you can try reading the story in Spanish only. Ask the children to say it with you. Ask them to read it only if they are eager to try. The spelling could be confusing and put them off.

- Above all, encourage the children to try it, and give lots of praise. Little children are usually quite unself-conscious and this is excellent for building up confidence in a foreign language.

First edition for the United States, its dependencies, Canada, and the Philippines published in 2006 by Barron's Educational Series, Inc. Text and illustrations © Copyright 2005 by b small publishing

Address all inquiries to:
Barron's Educational Series, Inc. • 250 Wireless Boulevard • Hauppauge, New York 11788 • **http://www.barronseduc.com**

ISBN-13: 978-0-7641-5873-5   ISBN-10: 0-7641-5873-2
Library of Congress Catalog Card Number 2005921559

Printed in China
9 8 7 6 5 4 3 2 1

George, the goldfish

Jorge, el pez dorado

Lone Morton

Pictures by Leighton Noyes
Spanish by Rosa María Martín

BARRON'S

Harry has a goldfish.
His name is George.

Harry tiene un pez dorado.
Se llama Jorge.

George swims around and around in his bowl. Harry loves to watch him.

Jorge nada y nada en su pecera.
A Harry le encanta mirarlo.

But one day Harry's goldfish dies.

Pero un día el pez dorado de Harry
se muere.

Harry is very sad and he cries.

Harry está muy triste y llora.

His mother hugs him.
"George made you happy."

Su madre le abraza.
"Jorge te hizo feliz".

"We will bury him in the garden," she says. "And he will make the garden happy."

"Lo enterraremos en el jardín", dice. "Y hará feliz al jardín".

Harry paints a small box.

Harry decora una cajita.

He puts George on some leaves
in the box.

Pone a Jorge sobre unas hojas
dentro de la caja.

It's summer.
Harry and his mother dig
a hole under the tree.

Es verano.
Harry y su madre hacen
un hoyo debajo de un árbol.

Harry puts the box in the hole
and covers it with earth.

Harry pone la caja en el hoyo
y la cubre con tierra.

His mother plants three flower bulbs.

Su madre planta tres bulbos de flores.

"Now George will help the garden to grow. Wait and see," says Harry's mother.

"Ahora Jorge ayudará al jardín a crecer. Espera y verás", dice la madre de Harry.

In the autumn, all the leaves fall from the tree.

En el otoño, todas las hojas caen del árbol.

In the winter, it is cold and it snows.

En el invierno, hace frío y nieva.

And then, in the spring, three little shoots appear.

Y entonces, en primavera, aparecen tres brotecitos.

Every day, they grow...
Cada día, crecen...

and grow...
y crecen...

and grow.
y crecen.

One morning, Harry looks out the window and sees three yellow flowers.

Una mañana, Harry mira por la ventana y ve tres flores amarillas.

Harry and his mother run out into the garden.

Harry y su madre corren al jardín.

"You see, George helped them to grow tall and beautiful," says his mother.

"Ves, Jorge las ayudó a crecer altas y bellas", dice su madre.

Harry smiles.

Harry sonríe.

Don't worry if your pronunciation isn't quite correct. The important thing is to be willing to try.

The pronunciation guide is based on the Spanish accent used in Latin America. Although it cannot be completely accurate, it certainly will be a great help.

• Read the guide as naturally as possible, as if it were English.

• Put stress on the letters in *italics*, as in *mah*-dreh

If you can, ask a Spanish-speaking person to help, and move on as soon as possible to speaking the words without the guide.

Note: Spanish adjectives usually have two forms, one for masculine and one for feminine nouns, as in **bello** and **bella** (see the next page).

Words Las palabras
lahs pah-*lah*-brahs

goldfish
el pez dorado

ehl pehs doh-*rah*-doh

mother
la madre

lah *mah*-dreh

tree
el árbol

ehl *ahr*-bohl

tall
alto/alta

ahl-toh/*ahl*-tah

leaf/leaves
la hoja/las hojas

lah *oh*-hah/lahs *oh*-hahs

flower
la flor

lah flohr

garden
el jardín

ehl hahr-*deen*

beautiful
bello/bella

beh-yoh/*beh*-yah

to grow
crecer

creh-*sehr*

happy
feliz

feh-*lees*

to smile
sonreír

sohn-reh-*eer*

sad
triste

trees-teh

to cry
llorar

yoh-*rahr*

spring
la primavera

lah pree-mah-veh-rah

summer
el verano

ehl veh-rah-noh

autumn
el otoño

ehl oh-ton-yoh

winter
el invierno

ehl een-vee-ehr-noh

cold
frío

free-oh

it snows
nieva

nee-eh-vah

A simple guide to pronouncing this Spanish story

Jorge, el pez dorado
hor-heh, ehl pehs do-*rah*-doh

Harry tiene un pez dorado.
hah-ree tee-*eh*-neh oon pehs do-*rah*-doh

Se llama Jorge.
seh *yah*-mah *hor*-heh

Jorge nada y nada en su pecera.
hor-heh *nah*-dah ee *nah*-dah ehn soo peh-*seh*-rah

A Harry le encanta mirarlo
ah *hah*-ree leh ehn-*kahn*-tah mee-*rahr*-loh

Pero un dia el pez dorado de Harry se muere.
peh-roh oon *dee*-ah ehl pehs do-*rah*-doh deh *hah*-ree seh *mweh*-reh

Harry está muy triste y llora.
hah-ree ehs-*tah* mwee *trees*-teh ee *yoh*-rah

Su madre le abraza.
soo *mah*-dreh leh ah-*brah*-sah

"Jorge te hizo feliz".
hor-heh teh *ee*-soh feh-*lees*

"Lo enterraremos en el jardin", dice.
loh ehn-tehr-rah-*reh*-mohs ehn ehl har-*deen*, *dee*-seh

"Y hará feliz al jardin".
ee ah-*rah* feh-*lees* ahl har-*deen*

Harry decora una cajita.
hah-ree deh-*koh*-rah oo-nah kah-*hee*-tah

Pone a Jorge sobre unas hojas dentro de la caja.
poh-neh ah *hor*-heh *soh*-breh oo-nahs *oh*-hahs *dehn*-troh deh lah *kah*-hah

Es verano.
ehs veh-*rah*-noh

Harry y su madre hacen un hoyo debajo de un árbol.
hah-ree ee soo *mah*-dreh ah-sehn oon *oh*-yoh deh-*bah*-hoh deh oon *ahr*-bohl

Harry pone la caja en el hoyo y la cubre con tierra.
hah-ree *poh*-neh lah *kah*-hah ehn ehl *oh*-yoh ee lah *koo*-breh kohn tee-*eh*-rah

Su madre planta tres bulbos de flores.
soo *mah*-dreh *plahn*-tah trehs *bool*-bohs deh *floh*-rehs

"Ahora Jorge ayudará al jardin a crecer.
ah-*hoh*-rah *hor*-heh ah-yoo-dah-*rah* ahl har-*deen* ah kreh-*sehr*

Epera y verás", dice la madre de Harry.
ehs-*peh*-rah ee veh-*rahs*, *dee*-seh lah *mah*-dreh deh *hah*-ree

En el otoño, todas las hojas caen del árbol.
ehn ehl oh-*tohn*-yoh, *toh*-dahs lahs *oh*-hahs kah-ehn dehl *ahr*-bohl

En el invierno, hace frío y nieva.
ehn ehl een-vee-*ehr*-noh, ah-seh *free*-oh ee nee-*eh*-vah

Y entonces, en primavera, aparecen tres brotecitos.
ee ehn-*tohn*-sehs, ehn pree-mah-*veh*-rah, ah-pah-*reh*-sehn trehs broh-teh-*see*-tohs

Cada dia, crecen, y crecen, y crecen.
kah-dah *dee*-ah, *kreh*-sehn, ee *kreh*-sehn, ee *kreh*-sehn

Una mañana, Harry mira por la ventana
oo-nah man-*yah*-nah, *hah*-ree *mee*-rah pohr lah vehn-*tah*-nah

y ve tres flores amarillas.
ee veh trehs *floh*-rehs ah-mah-*ree*-yahs

Harry y su madre corren al jardin.
hah-ree ee soo *mah*-dreh *koh*-rehn ahl har-*deen*

"Ves, Jorge las ayudó a crecer altas y bellas", dice su madre.
vehs, *hor*-heh lahs ah-yoo-*doh* ah kreh-*sehr* *ahl*-tahs ee *beh*-yahs, *dee*-seh soo *mah*-dreh

Harry sonríe.
hah-ree sohn-*ree*-eh